# KNOCK KNOCK JOKES

Compiled and Illustrated by
## Viki Woodworth

Distributed to Schools and Libraries
in Canada by
SAUNDERS BOOK COMPANY
Box 308
Collingwood, Ontario, Canada 69Y3Z7 / (800) 461-9120

Library of Congress Cataloging-in-Publication Data
Rothaus, James.
Knock-knock jokes / Jim Rothaus; compiled and illustrated by Viki Woodworth.
p. cm.
Summary: A collection of knock-knock jokes.
Example: Knock knock, Who's there? Atch. Atch who? Bless you!
ISBN 0-89565-729-5
1. Knock-knock jokes. 2. Wit and humor, Juvenile.
[1. Knock-knock jokes. 2. Jokes.]
I. Woodworth, Viki, ill.        II. Title.
PN6231.K55R68 1991              91-15966
818'.5402—dc20                  CIP / AC

# KNOCK KNOCK JOKES

Compiled and Illustrated by
**Viki Woodworth**

THE CHILD'S WORLD

**Knock knock.** Who's there?
**Zombies.** Zombies who?
**Zombies are after me.**


**Knock knock.** Who's there?
**Sam and Janet.** Sam and Janet, who?
**Sam and Janet evening.**


**Knock knock.** Who's there?
**Ben.** Ben who?
**Ben looking all over for you.**


**Knock knock.** Who's there?
**Amahl.** Amahl who?
**Amahl shook up.**


**Knock knock.** Who's there?
**Hominy.** Hominy who?
**Hominy times you gonna ask?**


**Knock knock.** Who's there?
**Ima.** Ima who?
**Ima sick of knocking. Let me in!**

**Knock knock.** Who's there?
**Goblin.** Goblin who?
**Goblin your food is bad for you.**

**Knock knock.**   Who's there?
**Freddy.**   Freddy who?
**Freddy or not, here I come.**


**Knock knock.**   Who's there?
**Dragon.**   Dragon who?
**Dragon your feet ruins your shoes.**


**Knock knock.**   Who's there?
**Emma.**   Emma who?
**Emma gonna go now.**


**Knock knock.**   Who's there?
**Who.**   Who who?
**What are you, an owl?**


**Knock knock.**   Who's there?
**Gucci.**   Gucci who?
**Gucci-gucci-goo.**


**Knock knock.**   Who's there?
**Fresno.**   Fresno who?
**Rudolph, the Fresno reindeer.**

**Knock knock.** Who's there?
**Sultan.** Sultan who?
**Sultan pepper are great spices.**

**Knock knock.** Who's there?
**Veal.** Veal who?
**Veal my head, I think I'm sick.**


**Knock knock.** Who's there?
**Wooden shoe.** Wooden shoe who?
**Wooden shoe be warmer with a sweater?**


**Knock knock.** Who's there?
**Tootle.** Tootle who?
**What, leaving so soon?**


**Knock knock.** Who's there?
**Holt.** Holt who?
**Holt your hands up. Give me all your money.**


**Knock knock.** Who's there?
**Alaska.** Alaska who?
**Alaska my mommy.**


**Knock knock.** Who's there?
**Atch.** Atch who?
**Bless you!**

**Knock knock.**   Who's there?
**Snowman.**   Snowman who?
**Snowman, it's a woman.**

**Knock knock.** Who's there?
**Lemmy.** Lemmy who?
**Lemmy some money, I'm broke.**


**Knock knock.** Who's there?
**Owl.** Owl who?
**Owl never tell.**


**Knock knock.** Who's there?
**Ida.** Ida who?
**Ida know.**


**Knock knock.** Who's there?
**Farm.** Farm who?
**Farm-e to know and you to find out.**


**Knock knock.** Who's there?
**Goat.** Goat who?
**Goat your room.**


**Knock knock.** Who's there?
**Duane.** Duane who?
**Duane the tub. It's too full.**

**Knock knock.**  Who's there?
**Gopher.**  Gopher who?
**Gopher a hike?**

**Knock knock.** Who's there?
**Vampire.** Vampire who?
**Vampire State Building.**


**Knock knock.** Who's there?
**Athena.** Athena who?
**Athena spaceship go by.**


**Knock knock.** Who's there?
**Luke.** Luke who?
**Luke through the window and you'll see.**


**Knock knock.** Who's there?
**Ice Cream Soda.** Ice Cream Soda who?
**Ice Cream Soda folks hear me!**


**Knock knock.** Who's there?
**Otis.** Otis who?
**Otis wonderful weather.**


**Knock knock.** Who's there?
**Elsie.** Elsie who?
**Elsie ya later, alligator.**

**Knock knock.** Who's there?
**Bat.** Bat who?
**Bat you can't wait for Christmas.**

**Knock knock.** Who's there?
**Abby.** Abby who?
**Abby birthday to you.**


**Knock knock.** Who's there?
**Ivan.** Ivan who?
**Ivan eye on you.**


**Knock knock.** Who's there?
**Distress.** Distress who?
**Distress is too short.**


**Knock knock.** Who's there?
**Nobel.** Nobel who?
**Nobel so I knocked.**


**Knock knock.** Who's there?
**Rhett.** Rhett who?
**Rhett-y or not, here I come.**


**Knock knock.** Who's there?
**Hewlette.** Hewlette who?
**Hewlette all the flies in?**

**Knock knock.** Who's there?
**Don Juan.** Don Juan who?
**Don Juan to study today.**

**Knock knock.** Who's there?
**Olaf.** Olaf who?
**Olaf you.**


**Knock knock.** Who's there?
**Rhoda.** Rhoda who?
**Rhoda cow once, have you?**


**Knock knock.** Who's there?
**Dustin.** Dustin who?
**Dustin is hard work!**


**Knock knock.** Who's there?
**Dutch.** Dutch who?
**Dutch me again an I'll pop you.**


**Knock knock.** Who's there?
**Leaf.** Leaf who?
**Leaf me alone.**


**Knock knock.** Who's there?
**Ida.** Ida who?
**If Ida knew you were coming, Ida baked a cake.**

**Knock knock.** Who's there?
**Rabbit.** Rabbit who?
**Rabbit up, it's a present.**

**Knock knock.**   Who's there?
**Diploma.**   Diploma who.
**Call Diploma, the sink's clogged.**


**Knock knock.**   Who's there?
**Scold.**   Scold who?
**Scold out here, let me in!**


**Knock knock.**   Who's there?
**Hook.**   Hook who?
**Hook cares?**


**Knock knock.**   Who's there?
**Adolf.**   Adolf who?
**Adolf ball just hit me in the mouf.**


**Knock knock.**   Who's there?
**Moscow.**   Moscow who?
**Moscow gives lots of milk.**


**Knock knock.**   Who's there?
**Wendy.**   Wendy who?
**Wendy wind blows, the cradle will rock.**

**Knock knock.** Who's there?
**Little Old Lady.** Little Old Lady who?
**I didn't know you could yodel.**

**Knock knock.** Who's there?
**Duet.** Duet who?
**Duet right or don't duet at all.**


**Knock knock.** Who's there?
**Hannah.** Hannah who?
**Hannah partridge in a pear tree.**


**Knock knock.** Who's there?
**Meyer.** Meyer who?
**Meyer in a nasty mood.**


**Knock knock.** Who's there?
**Freeze.** Freeze who?
**Freeze a jolly good fellow.**


**Knock knock.** Who's there?
**Weevil.** Weevil who?
**Weevil be going now.**


**Knock knock.** Who's there?
**Annie.** Annie who?
**Anybody home?**

**Knock knock.**  Who's there?
**Dracula.**  Dracula who?
**Dracula juice.**

**Knock knock.**  Who's there?
**Jamaica.**  Jamaica who?
**Jamaica cake for dessert?**


**Knock knock.**  Who's there?
**Sarah.**  Sarah who?
**Sarah doctor in the house?**


**Knock knock.**  Who's there?
**Ella.**  Ella who?
**Ella-mentary school is hard!**


**Knock knock.**  Who's there?
**Lettuce.**  Lettuce who?
**Lettuce in and you'll find out.**


**Knock knock.**  Who's there?
**Adam.**  Adam who?
**Adam my way! I'm comin' thru.**


**Knock knock.**  Who's there?
**Dot.**  Dot who?
**I dot my eyes on you.**

**Knock knock.** Who's there?
**Cook.** Cook who?
**Hey! Who are you calling cookoo?**

**Knock knock.**  Who's there?
**Ya.**  Ya who?
**I didn't know you'd be so glad to see me.**


**Knock knock.**  Who's there?
**Boo.**  Boo who?
**No need to cry, it's only a joke.**


**Knock knock.**  Who's there?
**Candy.**  Candy who?
**Candy-magine why you'd want to know.**


**Knock knock.**  Who's there?
**Mimi.**  Mimi who?
**Mimi at the corner and I'll show you.**


**Knock knock.**  Who's there?
**Bolivia.**  Bolivia who?
**Bolivia me, I understand.**


**Knock knock.**  Who's there?
**Value.**  Value who?
**Value be my Valentine?**

**Knock knock.**    Who's there?
**Weasel.**    Weasel who?
**Weasel while you work.**

**Knock knock.** Who's there?
**Norma Lee.** Norma Lee who?
**Norma Lee I don't knock, I just go in.**


**Knock knock.** Who's there?
**Juneau.** Juneau who?
**Juneau the way to New York?**


**Knock knock.** Who's there?
**Charlotte.** Charlotte who?
**Charlotte a stars out tonight.**


**Knock knock.** Who's there?
**Pasture.** Pasture who?
**Pasture bedtime, isn't it?**


**Knock knock.** Who's there?
**Osborn.** Osborn who?
**Osborn in Ohio.**


**Knock knock.** Who's there?
**Eddie.** Eddie who?
**Eddie body there?**

**Knock knock.**   Who's there?
**Ghosts.**   Ghosts who?
**Who ghosts there?**

**Knock knock.** Who's there?
**Dishes.** Dishes who?
**Dishes the police! Open up!**


**Knock knock.** Who's there?
**Shelby.** Shelby who?
**Shelby comin' round the mountain when she comes.**


**Knock knock.** Who's there?
**Dexter.** Dexter who?
**Dexter hall with boughs of holly.**


**Knock knock.** Who's there?
**Tim.** Tim who?
**Tim-ber!**


**Knock knock.** Who's there?
**Madison.** Madison who?
**Madison helps you get well.**


**Knock knock.** Who's there?
**Could She.** Could She who?
**Could She, could she coo.**

**Knock knock.** Who's there?
**Tarzan.** Tarzan who?
**Tarzan stripes forever.**

**Knock knock.**   Who's there?
**Butter.**   Butter who?
**Butter late than never.**


**Knock knock.**   Who's there?
**Tick.**   Tick who?
**Ticklish, are you?**


**Knock knock.**   Who's there?
**Beef.**   Beef who?
**Beefore I forget, your shoe is untied.**


**Knock knock.**   Who's there?
**Tank.**   Tank who.
**You're welcome.**


**Knock knock.**   Who's there?
**Ghana.**   Ghana who?
**Not Ghana take this anymore.**


**Knock knock.**   Who's there?
**Ohio.**   Ohio who?
**Ohio Silver.**

**Knock knock.** Who's there?
**Safari.** Safari who?
**Safari, so good.**

**Knock knock.**   Who's there?
**Europe.**   Europe who?
**Europe to no good, I can tell.**


**Knock knock.**   Who's there?
**Witch.**   Witch who?
**Witch way did they go?**


**Knock knock.**   Who's there?
**Roach.**   Roach who?
**Roach you a note, why didn't you write back?**


**Knock knock.**   Who's there?
**Philip.**   Philip who?
**Philip my glass, it's empty.**


**Knock knock.**   Who's there?
**Eve.**   Eve who?
**Eve you need me, just call.**


**Knock knock.**   Who's there?
**Hiss.**   Hiss who?
**Gesundheit.**